ILLOCALITY

ILLOCALITY

JOSEPH MASSEY

WAVE BOOKS

SEATTLE & NEW YORK

Published by Wave Books

www.wavepoetry.com

Copyright © 2015 by Joseph Massey

All rights reserved

Wave Books titles are distributed to the trade by

Consortium Book Sales and Distribution

Phone: 800-283-3572 / SAN 631-760X

Library of Congress Cataloging-in-Publication Data

Massey, Joseph.

[Poems. Selections]

Illocality / Joseph Massey. — First edition.

pages ; cm

ISBN 978-1-940696-14-0 (hardcover) —

ISBN 978-1-940696-15-7 (softcover)

I. Title.

PS3613.A81933A6 2015

811'.6—dc23

2014042286

Designed and composed by Quemadura

Printed in the United States of America

9 8 7 6 5 4 3 2 1

First Edition

Wave Books 052

ILLOCALITY

PARSE

Dawn marks the wall

a thin flange of
off-blue

An imagined
silence

Always an imagined
silence

The speed
at which sleep's
fogged dialogue withers

into the present
noun-scape

This rift valley

A volley of
seasonal beacons

Window
where mind

finds orbit

+

All a world can do
is appear

The window
intones

A room
whose walls

warp with sun

What's seen
is dreamed

We think
ourselves here

TURNED

A notch
at the top of the mountain—

the eye
without a thought

threads the sky through.

How hours take

the stain of hours
and hold beneath their bloom

these things arranged
to resemble a season.

Summer's hum and lag.

To walk into it—

breathe the frequencies
that knot the air, another

animal baffled
to be an animal.

YARD (THREE ANGLES)

In the indent of
a day: wagging
        ferns modulate
glass table glow

        gnats needle
light's surface
        a texture
warmth conjures

    +

        a bulge
in the overgrowth
        a shattered
ceramic toilet

                    field's far edge
          palpitates
                    pink ribbons
          tied to stumps

               +

                    squirrel-clatter
          caught in
                    unnamed tree's
          canopy

                    blue jay
          geometry
                    in the direction
          this reads

AFTER WITTGENSTEIN

A contrail divides the skyline
wrinkled with heat. Flies circle trash—
clear plastic—at the seam
between brick path and lawn.
Hours atrophy.

There *is* the inexpressible
but it doesn't show itself
today. It doesn't
show itself in summer.

Even shade as it erases
radiates.

ROUTE 31

Yellow centerline
split with roadkill.

First day of summer—I've got my omen—

the clouds are hollow, roving
above a parking lot.

Each strip-mall pennant blurred.

So much metal
shoving sun

the sun shoves back.

TO SURFACE

through interference

(the prestorm
pall, wind-
less—

> charged particles
> approaching
> *acoustic effect*)

with a word
in mind

and then another

with the mind set aside.

THIRD FLOOR

Peripheral forsythia uncinched—
a quincunx pattern—
around a bare foundation:
cement the same bloodless
color as this stretched-to-broken

sun. At the window
    a wasp—two wasps
swat the glare.

    +

How many weeks indoors

watching the lines
that cross, that stain
and form a field
from the field
I forgot, winter forgot.

+

Birdsong next door
slipknots construction noise.

The day has its ballast.

THE FRAME

Morning makes
shapes, re-
combines the
room. A blue
line over
a gray line—
the slippage
pinned to
a wall.
What the window
lets in.
What it lets out.
Weather
moving into
and out of
weather. How
sight splinters
vision, braces me

here—there.
From a swamp
where the road
dead-ends
life spools up
into un-
spooling
July haze.
A blue line
and a gray line.

A TITLE FOR THE HAZE

In a patch of sunlight
a decapitated grasshopper
twitches. The sunlight twitches.
Sky the size of a sky imagined.

Squint to see the quarter moon
—shallow gash on blue horizon.
Squint to hear beyond windows
wafting muzak. I'm half-awake

in this field of turned-on particulars.
A wreck of yellow blossoms
under a barn-door window.

A barn door without the barn.

CURTAINS

No silence
in the house.

No house
in silence.

Something's
always

mumbling,
stridulating

into dust—
the drift

of it—
which is

not a
song.

GREENFIELD

Neon sex-shop sign
levitates within brick.

Cloud ridge
brims purple
over shadow-
flattened mountain.
A transient

trips through
a fog of gnats

under a streetlamp, eyes
closed, licking the air.

From the center
of the inexplicable

night branches out.

ON MIGRATION

A split glyph
drags south
over a parking lot.

The suction
of dusk.
We watch it

wrest
margin
from margin.

Your face
in the half-light.

The aphasia
of the shape

of your face
in the half-light.

Autumn
embalms
the hour.

TAKE PLACE

It must be enough
to live in the variations

of wind alone.
To sing the seams.

Apprehended
by vision, we
think we've seen.

Gutted Sunday glow divided
by white and yellow
lines. Glass

crushed over asphalt—
the sparkle in a pothole.

No ideas
but in parking lots.

Grief ground down
to the bare sense of an I
imagining itself here.

Winter-chipped sidewalk
annotated by grass clippings

and bird shit
white as paint.

Phrase after phrase
falls into place, out of
place, rewriting a world.

Sight: a lengthening fracture.

A palette stammers
to assemble the landscape.

Rain claps
dead leaves.

In overgrown brush
a nameless animal's
short-circuited shriek.

A lucid dream
signals the new season.

All those flowering trees
rooted to graves.

Thin indentations
where language was—

toppled row of tombstones—

appear and reappear
under a long wave of grass.

When weather
won't say

the unsaid.
An exchange

between light and wind—

the way I'd want
a line to move
to carve space.

Light and wind,

and the objects
between them,

pronouncing
only themselves.

Between sidewalk and curb
tiger lilies flare and bend

—a shape that resembles
the shape of the thought
that found them
there.

As if a field guide
could prevent
the present

from disintegrating
around us.

Gasoline and honeysuckle
unravel the air. Air charged

with stridulation, echo-

location, what scatters at dusk
to scavenge and be scavenged.

A noun
staggers through
the gloam, the

indescribable
color

opening, closing.

The world is real
in its absence of a world.

AN INTERIM

Lines fade
and forms fold

into the singular

A diseased shrub

absorbs
the leftover glow—

the early dark—

in a parking lot

strewn with
seasonal debris

Highway's
bled-together
glare

chafes
an adjacent
field:

a simulacrum
of panic

Fields midfreeze flash past

At a red light an embankment filled with mud
fills my peripheral vision—picking up speed

the shine of a signpost washes it out

In motion the mind
burrows, wordless

before the next sentence unravels
bent by sun as it cuts through traffic

December
reverberates with decay
and the freezing over of decay

How the weather reads into you:

a phrase
at the back of the throat—

a phrase
that won't flower

                    Ice fastens
          caution tape (summer
                         wrung the yellow out)

          to weeds wrapped
                         around a mound of
          crushed cans

To speak, to point

To account for anything
in the drift

The weight—the weightlessness—of it

Snowscape snowswept
and the gravestones narrow as day narrows

These days need crows and so they come
A counterpoint to white

       unwinding white
over root and bone

A fast thaw
and now
the snow's
fog, those
low oval
knots waft-
ing into the
mountain, how
they stop at
the center
and hold
a pattern I
don't think
to think there

Street sign
and bare branch

reflected
in black ice

The cartography
of the cold

To stand outside of it

As if a world
were real

That anything isn't
      That anything *is*

A world erased:
      a world arranged

The sight of
a snow rut's
gullied
filth

(the slow
exchange
with pavement)
overwhelms

the want
to say what
floods now
above it

THE SPAN

in memory of Nancy Holt

                    Start with
          a map, a sheet
                    of paper

                         Thinking
               is site-specific

Glare rusting air—

the sightline
disrupted

"I remember

the quarry"

a blank

The color of rock
        —the color of decay

Perception's
      a process

Sky-mound
    at the bottom

of the hill's
    a swamp

A parking lot—
degrees of torpor

Day's figurations
fall slack
over asphalt

Broken glass   horizon

It's the fact of
this room: what's there
to say within the day's shape.

Sky divides to frame
a version of
a world.

Where we are:
where we're not.

Sun, a clipped syllable
drawn over
what weather's
disfigured.

Ice on the field
recedes. Something—

silver cellophane trash—
flares in the monochrome.

A kind of dream language
attenuates our per-
ception. How

the landscape lists

into chain-link,
parking lot, objects
barely held to their names.

SUGARLOAF

Sunset on sandstone cliff face
radiates red, blistered
red receding the moment
it's noticed

to limbs flayed so thin they drip—
calligraphic—over snowpack's
gray gradient.

Vertical clouds disrupt
the skyline's lateral
trajectory. The eye

unfocused draws inward
so only horizon
remains—radiant gash

the dark installs to trap.

DIAL

a row of icicles delineates the day

the shadow of a row of icicles on white stucco

POLAR LOW

Half-sheathed in ice
a yellow double-wide trailer

mirrors the inarticulate morning.
The amnesiac sun.

And nothing else
to contrast these variations of white

and thicket
choked by thicket

in thin piles that dim the perimeter.

Every other noun
frozen over.

CONTAIN

Those concatenated
husks of ice
that line the lawn's
edge, far-
lapping shadows
(narrow, as if
scratched into
week-old
snow's scum-
pocked surface).
Give the day
its sign, some
emblem, to
read our-
selves out
of past
into place. No
world without
delineation. No
thing until

detonated
into its word.
Carpenter ant
navigates a knot
on an elm stump
and vanishes
through a cavity
of rot. Sight
is lost to sight.
At the border
between seasons
air's grainy with
light's lengthening.
Listen to an hour
shift shape, how
it contains
sonic detritus
in a dream-thin
frame, slush
spun under tires,
a church bell's
high note
bent above
dusk folding
the corners in.

THAW COMPASS

attic garret dawn
time tuned to a tone   a color
warped Victorian window's
swollen glow sustains

alluvial horizon holds
a pattern   morning   a walk
down the block   blackened snowbank
and peripheral cemetery follow

skyline   mountain-locked
snaps setting
sun in
two

March rain snow thaw
crumpled metal sign stuck
gravel-grained mud   mulch
ground to dust over sidewalk divots

Thursday's ruins collect
in the recesses of a walk
even this washed-out waste
is history   is measure   to notice

false spring fibrous light
broadsides arkose sandstone
cliff face   the Connecticut
below throws silent lines of current

window snowscape   daybreak rebounds
6:43   the corners of the room curl blue
behind my head dreamed words
hum as they diffuse

cemetery stone blanked by weather
moss   thaw-dark   green gone
orange verging white
rough as coral to the eye

the mind
snagged in sound
of paper birch bark
flagging   whatever air is there

season's cusp's forms plunge
undone   undoing day
the wild all
all of this was

EASTER

it begins to brim
sideways

blare gray
rubbery sun

these things
that hung on

soundless
sieve

EASTER (2)

April shapes March mud
the bulk of

the backyard
squirrels plod   antique
junk pile   rust
articulates
rust

cold shadows map the day
behind curtains   in rhythm
with panic
wind around the attic rattles

half-shattered glass
sheet leans on rusted toaster
slots stuffed with mulch   yard's margins
spring rummages

April delirium
circumference of rot
riots color   winter-ripped thicket
dissipates dirt plume

train sound
trails in mind
Sunday reduced
to a syntax of dust

a world   this one
ignites on a word
and the landscape uncoils
hinged to a name   to a heap of dirt

paper birch backdrops
yellow willow metronome
stratocumulus muffles sun
the yard's the only news on

THIRD DAY

of spring
and flakes pattern air
with gray divots

revolving over
mud and shade. Now
sun: the runoff

from flattened
snowbanks
flickers. As if

weather could
measure desire.
Light strains

through objects—
adjusts the shape
of a world. Hear

and then see
a clear plastic strip
trapped in chain-link

spasm wind.

MARCH SATURATED

At a thought's
margin, phrases
splinter, litter breath.
Mudscape—

a given metaphor—
assembles the unsaid.

Ashen, angular
patches of ice
jut into so much
swamped geometry.

Let the day cohere

in the day's breakage
and mimic spring.

Gauzy sunburst
striping the thaw.

GAUGE

The color
of a thing
after it thaws
—raw, rusted.
April, a panic

pulls the field
apart, maps
the day in mud.
Long ruts of mud

and coruscated
edges where
runoff (so red
it's black) reflects
the sun-drift. There

flashes—*here*.
A wasp lands
on the page,

an unwritten phrase.

APRIL TALISMAN

Pluvial thrum of
peepers in the over-
  growth above a
vernal

    pool,
the sibilant
      scrim.

A landscape:

    a rhizome
of slant rhymes.

A mud dauber
          wobbles
    on the deck rail,

  draws noise
    to a point.

ILLOCALITY

To imagine a morning

the first
sounds from the street

and the house, its halls

scarifying
consciousness

Antique glass
smudges limbs

(more blue
than green)

flared out
over a roof

To imagine
the raw circumference

of a field
as it wakes

what we make of it

where our senses
send us

Gray oscillates gray
and the mountain

a line
lodged within it

gone slack at the end

No need
to mention
weather

The yard—
the measure

An unkempt
garden bed
convulses

synchronous
with traffic

flashing through
the fence

Stone bench
in a ring of weeds

Shadows ring—
a sound

Bees doused in
viscous sun,
erased

THE COURSE

All that wasn't
said—the half-said—

each fluorescent
stammer—

condensed
at this dead end

to forsythia's
rhythm

Thanks to Pepper Luboff for "In the indent of / a day . . ."

Ludwig Wittgenstein: "There is indeed the inexpressible. This *shows* itself; it is the mystical."

"An Interim" borrows a line ("Days need birds and so they come") from James Schuyler's "Hymn to Life."

"The Span" was written while listening to a lecture by Nancy Holt, recorded on October 5, 2013 at Princeton University.

"Easter" 1 and 2 both borrow a few words from Clark Coolidge's *Quartz Hearts*.

I first encountered the word "illocality" in Emily Dickinson's "A nearness to Tremendousness" (#963 in the *Complete Poems of Emily Dickinson*, edited by Thomas H. Johnson).

ACKNOWLEDGMENTS

Some versions of these poems first appeared in maga-
zines and journals: "Curtains," "On Migration," "Turned,"
The Account. "Parse," "The Span," *The Cultural Society.*
"The Frame," "Third Floor," *Hidden City Quarterly.*
"A Title for the Haze," "March Saturated," *Matter.*
"Route 31," "To surface," "Yard (Three Angles),"
Petri Press. "January Sheaf," *The Pinch.*

"Thaw Compass" initially appeared as a chapbook via
PressBoardPress.

Tungsten Press produced a broadside as well as a folio of
"Route 31" and published "An Interim" as a chapbook.

Thanks to Steven Fama, Peter Gizzi, Jacqueline Winter
Thomas, Kate Colby, Joshua Beckman and everyone at
Wave Books for their support and guidance.